The Unity Of All Life In Alchemy

A. S. Raleigh

Kessinger Publishing's Rare Reprints

Thousands of Scarce and Hard-to-Find Books on These and other Subjects!

- Americana
- Ancient Mysteries
- Animals
- Anthropology
- Architecture
- Arts
- Astrology
- Bibliographies
- Biographies & Memoirs
- Body, Mind & Spirit
- Business & Investing
- Children & Young Adult
- Collectibles
- Comparative Religions
- Crafts & Hobbies
- Earth Sciences
- Education
- Ephemera
- Fiction
- Folklore
- Geography
- Health & Diet
- History
- Hobbies & Leisure
- Humor
- Illustrated Books
- Language & Culture
- Law
- Life Sciences
- Literature
- Medicine & Pharmacy
- Metaphysical
- Music
- Mystery & Crime
- Mythology
- Natural History
- Outdoor & Nature
- Philosophy
- Poetry
- Political Science
- Science
- Psychiatry & Psychology
- Reference
- Religion & Spiritualism
- Rhetoric
- Sacred Books
- Science Fiction
- Science & Technology
- Self-Help
- Social Sciences
- Symbolism
- Theatre & Drama
- Theology
- Travel & Explorations
- War & Military
- Women
- Yoga
- *Plus Much More!*

**We kindly invite you to view our catalog list at:
http://www.kessinger.net**

THIS ARTICLE WAS EXTRACTED FROM THE BOOK:

Science of Alchemy

BY THIS AUTHOR:

A. S. Raleigh

ISBN 1564590070

LESSON V

The Unity of Life

9. For as the many motions of them [all] are different, and as their bodies are not like, yet has one speed been ordered for them all, it is impossible that there should be two or more makers for them.

For that one single order is not kept among "the many"; but rivalry will follow of the weaker with the stronger, and they will strive.

And if the maker of the lives that suffer change and death, should be another, he would desire to make the deathless ones as well; just as the maker of the deathless ones, [to make the lives] that suffer death.

But come! if there be two, if Matter's one, and Soul is one, in whose hands would there be the distribution for the making? Again, if both of them have some of it, in whose hands may there be the greater part?

For as the many motions of them [all] are different, and as their bodies are not like, yet has one speed been ordered for them all, it is impossible that there should be two or more makers for them.

The argument that was introduced in the preceding paragraph of the Text is continued here. First of all, the many motions of all the lives in Cosmos are different. Second, their bodies are not alike, but all of the different kinds of lives have different kinds of bodies; yet, notwithstanding this, one speed has been ordered for them all. By one speed being ordered for them, we are to understand that the Order of the Intelligible Cosmos has ordered this speed, in the sense of forcibly establishing that speed in their movements. Do not be confused by this expression speed, it has the meaning of Rhythm or Wave Motion; it does not mean that the diverse lives move with equal rapidity, but rather that there is a certain wave of moving Force that carries all of the lives with it, something similar to the expression, the Life Wave in some Occult Literature. What he means to teach is that, far from these lives moving by reason of their own force, the Life Wave or Stream of Motion is in each of them, and they are moved by the motive power of that Wave of Motion, hence it is said that they all have one speed, that of the Life Wave. We may illustrate this matter by looking at the three motions of the Earth. The Earth revolves every day, likewise once a year, it completely revolves around the Sun, turning completely upon its axis, and once in a Great Year of nearly twenty-five thousand nine hundred years, it makes the circuit of the Twelve Constellations. Now, we may compare the motions of the diverse lives to the Diurnal Motion of the Earth, and the diverse streams of lives to the Annular Motion of the Earth, but this one speed of all moving lives to the motion of the Earth during the Great Year. Now, this one speed that has been ordered for all the lives, being the speed at which they are alike moved by the Force of the Æon through the Intelligible Cosmos, is in no sense influenced by the diversity of the bodies, or the diversity of their several motions, but acts upon them all alike, it must therefore, be something *other* than the composition of their bodies, or the motions of their souls, and as it is but one speed, and hence but one motion, it is impossible that there should be two or more such motions. This is true, because if there were two or more such motions, then they would move the lives in two or more diverse rates of speed. It must be that as they are ordered by but one speed, there is but one to order this one speed, hence there is but one maker for them, and not two or more makers, seeing that two or more makers could not order the one speed. If there be but one speed, it follows that but one speed has been ordered, and if this be true, but one Order is ordering them, and this being true, there is but the one Maker, ordering them with that one Order. Thus it will follow that there is but the one maker for them all.

For that one single order is not kept among "the many"; but rivalry will follow of the weaker with the stronger, and they will strive.

He means to say the many do not agree among themselves, but rather there is rivalry, and striving for mastery. He is teaching that there is no such thing as willing cooperation in the ranks of the many, but that each one wants the preeminence over some one else, and hence, there is perpetual striving, the one against the other. Therefore, there can never be any such thing as order grown out of the many. His idea is that when order is found among the many, it is not an order developed among them, but rather an order established among them by reason of a power greater than the power of the many, which forces the many to submit to it. Hence, the very existence of order among the many, demonstrates that they are controlled by some power stronger than they are themselves. We see here another illustration of the utter contempt which the Hermetic Logos has ever had for every form of Democracy. The Democratic idea is that the many will express their opinion, and what ever opinion the majority hold to, this will be accepted by the others, and all will be perfectly willing to yield their opinions and their wills to the opinion and the will of the majority. Now, as a matter of fact, such a condition is utterly impossible. The majority may agree on a certain course, and the minority, for fear of being assaulted by the majority, may submit to that course, but they are of the same opinion that they were before. Government is founded as a means

THE SCIENCE OF ALCHEMY 81

of forcing the minority to submit to the will of the majority. It is for that reason that we have policemen and soldiers. The police power of a nation is the power that forces the individual to obey the laws rather than to follow his own opinions. Of course as a rule, the will of the majority is thwarted, because they elect men to office, who do not do what the people want them to do, but what they themselves want to do. Practical politics consists in the art of getting yourself elected to Congress to represent the majority, when you are in reality of the minority, and there enacting laws that are contrary to the wishes of the majority which you pretend to represent. There is never any such thing as the many reaching of themselves a common ground of action, there will in all cases be rivalry and strife. A policy never emanated from the masses. When they vote it is for the candidates rather than for their policies, it is the tendency of the biped sheep to follow leaders that enables a few men to govern them, hence all government is essentially Aristocratic and never in any sense of the word Democratic. He is holding that it is not in the nature of lives to agree, but that it is the nature of each one to seek the expression of his will, and in all of his relations with other lives, he will seek to dominate them. This is the nature of every one of the lives, hence, the many can never agree, seeing that it is a struggle in which each one is fighting with all the rest. This being true, order can never be established among the many if it has to come from the many. There can only be order among the many, when there is a will so strong that none of them can resist it, establishes its power over them, and coerces them all to obey it, and this must be the will of a single being. Autocracy must, therefore, be the only form of government capable of establishing order. He teaches, therefore, that the maker of the lives must literally make them obey him, otherwise there can be no order. Therefore, if there is order among the lives in Cosmos it is because the force of a single maker has determined their several courses, and they have not the power to do otherwise. In a word, none of them have Free Will but on the other hand, the wills of all of them are determined by a higher power than themselves. This is the Hermetic idea of the Cosmos, all lives are under the control of One superior Force, which they are unable to resist. Now the Hermetic Political Economy was similar to this. In the Hermetic view, the King is one in whom the Order of Cosmos is incarnate, to such an extent as to control all of the motions of his soul and spirit. In his case therefore, this Order takes the form of will, so that his will is ordered by the Order of Cosmos, hence he has the Cosmic will and not an individual will. Now it is to be borne in mind that in this view, will is the will-force, and not merely volition, the latter being an act of the will-force. We are then to understand that the Cosmic Order becomes will-force in the will of the King, and that he has no will in any other sense than this. The Majesty of the King. In this view the King is will-force, that impresses that will upon his subjects, to such an extent that their will is conditioned by it. In a word, his subjects are passible to the passion of the Royal Will. It moves them, and they are moved by it. The King's Majesty is that energy of his, by which and with which, his subjects are energized, so that they automatically express it in action. It is in this way that they are ordered by the Majesty of the King. In this view the King is never one of the people, but rather the focal point of the Order of Cosmos, a point in which all of this Order is focused, and where it becomes Majesty, or controlling will-force, which acting upon the people, conditions and determines their actions, so that the King is at all times obeyed. This power is the Majesty of the King. His Highness is that Higher Quality of his Life-force that gives him a greater dynamic power than any of his subjects and thereby enables him to transmute the wills of his subjects in harmony with his own. His Grace is that quality of his Force that enters into his subjects and thereby conditions them so as to make them better, not through fear, but through giving them a superior quality of will-force. Thus the King becomes a sort of god to his subjects, determining their conduct through the action of his Majesty, refining their qualities through the action of his Highness, and transmuting their will to a better state through the action of his Grace. Such men were termed Spiritual Kings because they ruled the spirits of their subjects and their bodies through their spirits. Such were indeed and in truth, Divine Kings. It is for this reason that Hermes contends that it is from the King that Order is established in a State. The order established by such a King, is a divine order, and is in no sense of the word human. It is such kings as these that can do no wrong, because their Majesty establishes order and justice among men. As the will of the King is not human but divine, it is at all times correct. At the same time it must be borne in mind that the people do not obey the King out of choice, but because they have no means of disobeying him, their conduct being determined by his Majesty. The subject, being energized by the Majesty of the king, acts according to such energizing. Whoever, has the Majesty to energize the people so as to determine their conduct is the King of those people, it makes no difference what name he bears. Thus it is that Order never originates among the many, but in every instance, it emanates from one, and enters into the many as individuals, ordering their conduct with its Order.

And if the maker of the lives that suffer change and death, should be another, he would desire to make the deathless ones as well; just as the maker of the deathless ones, [to make the lives] that suffer death.

He has indicated that a single order is never preserved among the many, but that, on the contrary, there will be rivalry and striving among them for the preeminence, hence a single order can come only from a single maker. Now, he goes on with the argument, and says, suppose there were two makers, one to make the deathless lives, and another to make the lives subject to death? What would be the result? Could they cooperate and thus work in harmony, each one doing his own work without interfering with the work of the other? Nay, the one who made the lives subject to death, would scorn the idea that the other maker was able to do a better work than he could do, therefore, he would not tolerate the idea that he should make the lives subject to death and then content himself to see his rival make more excellent lives. On the contrary, he would insist on making deathless lives as well, and would undertake to show that he could make lives superior to those his rival was able to make. Likewise, the maker of the deathless lives, would never be content to make them, and leave the work of making the lives subject to death, to his rival. He would say, as I have made the deathless lives, it of course follows that I have more ability in the art of making lives than has this rival of mine, who can only make lives that are subject to death. As the greatness of an immortal life transcends that of a mortal life, so does my greatness as a maker of lives transcend the greatness of this rival of mine, who can make only mortal lives, but is unable to confer upon them immortality. Therefore, he would say, I can make much better mortal lives than this rival of mine, therefore, he must stop this foolishness, and permit me to do all of the making. The natural rivalry between the two makers, would of necessity lead to two rival creations, and hence there would be eternal strife in the universe and hence no Cosmos or Order. Therefore, the fact that we have a Cosmos and not a Chaos, proves that there is but the one maker, of the lives subject to death and the deathless lives as well.

But come! if there be two,—if Matter's one, and Soul is one, in whose hands would there be the distribution for the making? Again, if both of them have some of it, in whose hands may there be the greater part?

Now the question of the two makers is reduced to the question of Matter and Soul as the two makers. Some might contend that material things, that is, bodies, were made by Matter unassisted by any other maker; and that souls were made by Soul, unassisted by any other maker. If this be the case; if Soul makes souls without reference to the bodies that are being made by Matter, and Matter makes bodies without reference to the souls that are being made by Soul, then in whose hands would be the distribution of Soul and Matter for the making? The difficulty is that if Matter followed her own caprice in making bodies, and Soul followed her own caprice in making souls, who would determine the number of souls that were made by Soul, and the number of bodies that were made by Matter? Is it reasonable to suppose that, each making without reference to the other maker's makings, there would be an exactly equal number of souls and bodies made? Would there not be the danger of souls being made for which there were no bodies, or bodies being made for which there were no souls? Or would there not be the danger of Matter making too many deathless bodies, and not enough bodies subject to death, or the reverse? And Soul making too many immortal souls and not enough mortal souls, or the reverse? You can see at a glance how complicated is the problem, and the absolute necessity of the work of Soul and Matter absolutely coinciding in the diverse types that they made in their work of making souls and bodies. But, what is to determine their doing this? What is to prevent a lot of work that is not in harmony and therefore abortive? Suppose this distribution is in the hands of both Soul and Matter, which exercises the greater control over the other? In either case, the one will be to an extent interfering with the other. Does Matter force Soul to make souls to suit its bodies? Or does Soul force Matter to make bodies suitable for its souls? We are absolutely forced to the conclusion that the distribution is not in the hands either of Soul or Matter, but that it is in the hands of some maker that is higher than either Soul or Matter, and one that is wholly One. Nay, rather are we forced to conclude that neither is Soul or Matter the maker, but rather that they are both used by the maker, Soul being the *materia* out of which he makes souls, and Matter the *materia* out of which he makes bodies, while he himself is above both Matter and Soul and is Ruler over both of them. This maker must be one who is wholly One, and who is able to express his Unity through the Duality of forces that he makes use of in his making.

10. But thus conceive it, then; that every living body doth consist of soul and matter, whether [that body be] of an immortal, or a mortal, or an irrational [life].

For that all living bodies are ensouled; whereas, upon the other hand, those that live not, are matter by itself.

And, in like fashion, Soul when in its self is, after its own maker, cause of life; but *the* cause of all life is He who makes the things that cannot die.

Her. How, then, is it that, first, lives subject unto death are other than the deathless ones? And, next, how is it that that Life which knows no death, and maketh deathlessness, doth not make animals immortal?

But thus conceive it, then; that every living body doth consist of soul and matter, whether [that body be] of an immortal, or a mortal, or an irrational [life].

There is as to their consistency, no difference between the bodies of immortal, mortal and irrational lives, in either case, if the body be alive, it is made up of soul and matter, the two must enter into it if it is to live. From this we are to understand that the constituent principles of the bodies of the immortals, of mortal lives and of the irrational animals are the same, they being made up of soul and matter. Hence, a god, a daimon, a genus, must have a body, and cannot live without it, and that body must be material. In like manner, a bird, a fish, a reptile, an insect or an animal must have a soul, and cannot live without it. All living things then must have material bodies and souls. There is here absolutely no distinction between them. A living body then is matter and soul in a state of union, that is matter ensouled by soul.

For that all living bodies are ensouled; whereas, on the other hand, those that live not, are matter by itself.

We are here distinctly informed that matter separate from soul can have no life, hence it is soul that makes matter to live. In a body of un-ensouled matter there will be no life, hence it follows that any living body, lives because of its soul. This shows that there is a soul in every living body, no matter how low in the scale of life it may be. The discussion as to whether the animals have souls or not is absurd, any living animal has a soul, and is alive because of its soul, whereas, a dead animal has no soul, and for that reason it is dead. To live is the equivalent of being ensouled, and likewise to be ensouled is the same as being alive. What ever lives then, is ensouled. There can be no life in matter separate from soul.

And, in like fashion, Soul when in its self is, after its own maker, cause of life; but *the* cause of all life is He who makes the things that cannot die.

By Soul being in its self, we are to understand Soul separate from Matter. Now, Soul while in this condition of separation from Matter is after its own maker, that is, in a subordinate condition to its own maker, the cause of life to bodies. That is to say, when Soul is joined to matter, it makes matter live by ensouling it. However, soul does not do this of her own volition, but under the compulsion of her maker, who is, therefore, the real cause of her ensouling matter and making it to live. The cause of all life however, the ultimate cause of all life is He who makes the things that cannot die. In other words, it is the maker of the souls themselves. He is the maker of the immortal lives, and through his making, bodies are made to live through their being ensouled by souls.

Her. How, then, is it that, first, lives subject unto death are other than the deathless ones? And, next, how is it that that Life which knows no death, and maketh deathlessness, does not make animals immortal?

Hermes introduces two questions here. First of all, how is it that lives subject unto death are other than the deathless ones? And second, if all lives are made by that Life which knows no death, and makes the deathless lives, why does it not make the animals immortal? Turning first to the first question: What is it that renders the mortal lives *other* than the immortal lives? Where is the line of demarcation to be drawn between the mortal and the immortal lives? What is it specifically that determines the mortality of the one, and the immortality of the other? We have seen how it is that all lives without any distinction whatever are composed of soul and matter; that all living bodies are such because matter has been ensouled, and that matter apart from soul is in all cases dead. This being the case, a mortal life has soul the same as an immortal life, and so does an immortal life contain the material body the same as does the mortal life. Now, seeing that they alike have bodies, and alike have souls; what is there in the life subject to death to determine its mortality? And in the deathless life, what is there to determine its immortality? There seems to be no distinction between them, what is it that constitutes one deathless, and the other subject to death. The second question renders the problem still more difficult of solution. A life is the result of the union of soul and matter, and of nothing else apparently, and they are the same in the case of both the mortal and the immortal life. Now, the maker of both the deathless lives, and the lives subject to death, is that Life which knows no death. Seeing that all the making is done by a maker who is Himself deathless, and who makes deathlessness, and is the maker of the deathless lives, how does He make the animals mortal rather than immortal. We have seen how it is that there is no distinction in the elements used, that is, soul and matter, now, if soul and matter are alike used by the maker of all lives; and if the nature of that maker is deathlessness, how can deathlessness, working through soul and matter, make some lives immortal and other mortal? How is it that the deathlessness of that Life enters into some of the things He makes, and not into others? This is the difficulty that is presented unto us, and it is essential that we should understand this; for if we understand this problem, we will have understood the essential distinction between mortal and immortal life; and thereby, will we understand the nature of the Gate between the two, and this is the most vital of all the questions connected with the Science of Alchemy. If there be some way by which we may bridge over the chasm between mortality and immortality, above all things, we want to find it out. If there is such a thing as Flesh Immortality to be attained, it will be through this secret that its attainment will be possible, and not otherwise.

This is the end of this publication.

Any remaining blank pages are for our book binding requirements and are blank on purpose.

To search thousands of interesting publications like this one, please remember to visit our website at:

http://www.kessinger.net

CPSIA information can be obtained
at www.ICGtesting.com
Printed in the USA
BVHW040347070422
633559BV00004B/530